VIRTUES FOR DISCIPLES

FORGIVENESS
Choosing to Receive and to Give

Virginia Herbers

D1548294

Little Rock
Scripture Study

LITURGICAL PRESS
Collegeville, Minnesota

www.littlerockscripture.org

Nihil obstat: Jerome Kodell, OSB, *Censor Librorum.*
Imprimatur: ✢ Anthony B. Taylor, Bishop of Little Rock, June 28, 2019.

Cover design by Ann Blattner. Photo courtesy of Getty Images.

Photos/illustrations: Pages 6, 9, 11, 12, 18, 22, 25, 30, 32, 34, Getty Images. Page 8, Monica Bokinskie. Page 16, Lightstock. Page 28, Joe Reish. Used with permission.

ISBN: 978-0-8146-6399-8 (print); 978-0-8146-6400-1 (e-book)

Contents

Introduction

Alive in the Word brings you resources to deepen your understanding of Scripture, offer meaning for your life today, and help you to pray and act in response to God's word.

Use any volume of **Alive in the Word** in the way best suited to you.

- **For individual learning and reflection,** consider this an invitation to prayerfully journal in response to the questions you find along the way. And be prepared to move from head to heart and then to action.
- **For group learning and reflection,** arrange for three sessions where you will use the material provided as the basis for faith sharing and prayer. You may ask group members to read each chapter in advance and come prepared with questions answered. In this kind of session, plan to be together for about an hour. Or, if your group prefers, read and respond to the questions together without advance preparation. With this approach, it's helpful to plan on spending more time for each group session in order to adequately work through each of the chapters.

- **For a parish-wide event or use within a larger group,** provide each person with a copy of this volume, and allow time during the event for quiet reading, group discussion and prayer, and then a final commitment by each person to some simple action in response to what he or she learned.

This volume on the topic of forgiveness is one of several volumes that explore **Virtues for Disciples**. Each of us is called to be a disciple, a follower of Christ. The life of a disciple is challenging, but it is the most fulfilling way to live. Called by name by the God who created us, we are shaped by the teachings of Christ and continually guided by the Holy Spirit. As we grow more deeply into this identity as disciples of Jesus Christ, we discover the valuable virtues that mark God's people.

Assurance of God's Forgiveness

Begin by asking God to assist you in your prayer and study. Then read through Psalm 130, a prayer of penance in the presence of God.

Psalm 130
[1]Out of the depths I call to you, LORD;
[2]Lord, hear my cry!
May your ears be attentive
to my cry for mercy.
[3]If you, LORD, keep account of sins,
Lord, who can stand?
[4]But with you is forgiveness
and so you are revered.

⁵I wait for the LORD,
my soul waits
and I hope for his word.
⁶My soul looks for the Lord
more than sentinels for daybreak.
More than sentinels for daybreak,
⁷let Israel hope in the LORD,
For with the LORD is mercy,
with him is plenteous redemption,
⁸And he will redeem Israel
from all its sins.

After a few moments of quiet reflection on the passage, consider the following background information provided in "Setting the Scene."

Setting the Scene

Forgiveness is a central tenet of our Judeo-Christian faith and an integral characteristic of a personal relationship with God. We profess that God is loving and forgiving, and we believe that God calls us to be people of forgiveness when we have been wronged. Whether hearing the Old Testament stories of Joseph forgiving his brothers (Gen 45) and God forgiving David (2 Sam 12:13), or Jesus' instruction to forgive "not seven times but seventy-seven times" (Matt 18:21-22), Scripture is filled with passages about forgiveness.

The psalms function as a "prayer book" for the people of Israel and for the church. Totaling one hundred fifty, the psalms in all their variety express every emotion possible in the relationship

between God and God's people—some psalms are filled with gratitude, others with pleas for help, and still others with cries of pain or sorrow.

Psalm 130 is a penitential psalm, a song of lament in which the psalmist acknowledges a personal need for God and pleads with the Lord for forgiveness. Inherent in the psalm is not only an admission of guilt but also a firm confidence that God will hear the penitent's cries and respond with forgiveness. After seeking the Lord with hope and waiting on the revelation of God's presence, the psalmist expresses a strong faith that the Lord's steadfast love will be what redeems him despite his own faults and failings.

The experience of fault and forgiveness expressed in Psalm 130 is familiar. We who know our own limitations likewise know God's infinite mercy. It is this firm conviction—both of our neediness and of God's abundance—that allows us to seek forgiveness from God, even from "out of the depths."

Psalm 130 will be considered a few verses at a time for a deeper understanding. The questions in the margins are intended for group discussion, personal reflection, or journaling.

Understanding the Scene Itself

¹Out of the depths I call to you, LORD;
²Lord, hear my cry!
May your ears be attentive
to my cry for mercy.

The psalmist begins this song with geo-graphical language. He identifies himself as being in the depths of the abyss, feeling far removed from God and needing to cry out loud in order to be heard. This lament is not a whimper or a still, small voice of pain. It is a cry, an entreaty that seeks a hearing from the Lord. The soul's desperation is evident, and the utter need for God to listen is made plain. This is no feeble request, no tentative petition; this is a full-throated plea looking for reception and receptivity.

The mere utterance of this cry demonstrates the psalmist's faith and hope in God. To plead for a hearing from God paradoxically implies a belief that God has already heard the plea to listen. The psalmist relies on the promise of Psalm 34, that

Call to mind a time when you have felt yourself in "the depths" and far distant from God due to your own poor choices. How did your soul cry out to God?

"the eyes of the LORD are directed toward the righteous and his ears toward their cry," and that God will answer those who seek him, delivering them from all their fears. The request for God to listen, then, is already an act of faith.

When we are in "the depths," it is likely God's absence that we experience most strongly, and we cry out from the deepest parts of our souls. Even in the felt experience of absence, however, we express our faith in God's presence by the very act of crying out. If we truly believed that God was absent, our cries would be pointless, mere expressions of pain and despair. It is in addressing our cries to God that our faith is expressed, even from places of misery and pain.

What experiences in your life have revealed some level of trust in God's presence even when you felt God's absence at the same time?

³If you, LORD, keep account of sins,
Lord, who can stand?
⁴But with you is forgiveness
and so you are revered.

Our attention turns away from the psalmist now and lands squarely on the Lord. Who is this God whom we worship? This is a God who does not mark our sins or count our failings; this God not only "has" forgiveness or "gives" forgiveness but *is* forgiveness; our God is revered and literally adore-able because he is a God who forgives.

In Hebrew, the wording in the third verse of the psalm, "who can stand," is harmonic with the phrase in the first verse, "out of the depths." Only when we rely on the forgiveness of God can the disharmonies of our life choices be resolved into an ability to rise up again and worship rightly.

God's willingness *not* to mark our sins is what allows us to take our rightful place, standing before him in worship. We revere God not because of *our* worthiness but because of God's.

In verse 4, the Hebrew word *hasselîhāh* is translated as "forgiveness" in English. This is the only place in the entirety of the Bible where this particular word is used, and the connotation is that the power to forgive is a power that belongs solely to God. One translation of verse 4 is "Yours is the power to forgive, / so that You may be held in awe" (*The Jewish Study Bible*, edited by Adele Berlin and Marc Zvi Brettler). For God to choose to forgive our sins, then, is for God to choose *us*, to choose a renewed relationship with us despite our sins. It means that God exercises the divine option to not "keep account" of our sins, which would add up to condemnation; rather, God chooses to forgive us. This choice leaves us, the forgiven ones, in a position of reverence for God's unfathomable goodness.

⁵I wait for the LORD,
my soul waits
and I hope for his word.
⁶My soul looks for the Lord
more than sentinels for daybreak.

Call to mind a time when God felt distant, not because of your own choices but simply because God's presence was not perceivable. What helped you to "keep watch" for the return of God's presence?

Having expressed firm faith in God's mercy, the psalmist now returns to his own experience—one that remains an experience of God's absence. The promise of God's forgiveness is sure, but the return of God's felt presence has not yet occurred, and so he waits. His cry has been uttered; he believes it has been heard because of his firm confidence in who God is, and now he waits on the response of the Lord.

The psalmist characterizes this waiting as a time of hope but also with the language of vigil. "My soul looks for the Lord / more than sentinels for daybreak." Those who keep night watch are eager for the first streaks of dawn, longing for the end of the darkness and the coming of the new day. This has undertones of the experience of the "rising Son" that was the event of Christ's resurrection, wherein the first rays of dawn manifested the empty tomb (see Luke 24:1).

Those who keep night vigils know that the morning is coming; it is only a matter of time. The arrival of the Lord is inevitable, so the psalmist waits in hope and longing. No matter how long the wait, no matter how dark the night, morning comes as a promise to every soul who waits for the Lord.

How has a previous experience of God's forgiveness bolstered your hope today?

More than sentinels for daybreak,
⁷let Israel hope in the LORD,
For with the LORD is mercy,
with him is plenteous redemption,
⁸And he will redeem Israel
from all its sins.

The soul's hope in the Lord is not a personal hope only; it is a hope for the entire people of God. "Let Israel hope in the Lord!" This redemption is not just for the penitent individual; this redemption is for all the people of Israel, who have no hope save the hope provided by God's forgiveness. Israel's history gives ample evidence of the chosen people's faithfulness but also many occasions of violating the covenant qualities of mercy, justice, and righteousness. The prophets of Israel raised awareness of this collective sinfulness, calling the community to cry out to God for forgiveness.

It is precisely the steadfast love of the Lord that is our hope and our shield as well, and it is the love and forgiveness of God alone that saves. In the book of Lamentations, we read: "The LORD's acts of mercy are not exhausted, / his compassion is not spent; / They are renewed each morning— / great is your faithfulness! / The LORD is my portion, I tell myself, / therefore I will hope in him" (Lam 3:22-24).

Just as Israel felt the weight of her sins, so does the church. How might the church seek God's forgiveness and in what areas?

God's love for his people is what prompts his forgiveness of our sins. The full strength of God's redemptive power is demonstrated in the gentleness of his response to our iniquities. And all Israel, all those chosen by God for union with himself, all the ends of the earth shall see the saving power of God (see Isa 52:10).

Praying the Word / Sacred Reading

Plumb the depths of your life experiences to name those areas that still need forgiveness from God. Rather than dwelling on your own mistakes, faults, or sins, turn your gaze to God, and hear the words of forgiveness that come from God's word: "For with the LORD is mercy, / with him is plenteous redemption."

Receive these words into your mind, let your breathing become deeper, and repeat the words slowly and continuously until you feel a greater stillness of spirit.

Consider putting these words somewhere you will see them multiple times each day: on a bathroom mirror, over the kitchen sink, or as wallpaper on your phone's home screen, etc.

Living the Word

Receiving God's forgiveness is a beautiful concept with which to pray but can be difficult to live. Sometimes the shame of owning our sinfulness prevents us from opening up to God's forgiveness. Sometimes our fear of punishment paralyzes us and keeps our relationship with God very shallow.

- *This week, try to identify a time in your past when you had a genuine experience of feeling God's love for you.*
- *Spend a few minutes just soaking in that experience of love, absorbing the warmth of it. Rather than contrast that with your own sinfulness, just bask in the truth of who God is without focusing on yourself at all.*
- *Keep your gaze locked on God.*

Forgiving as Jesus Forgives

Begin by asking God to assist you in your prayer and study. Then read the following passage from John 8, the story of Jesus, the woman caught in adultery, and those gathered to stone her.

John 8:3-11

³Then the scribes and the Pharisees brought a woman who had been caught in adultery and made her stand in the middle. ⁴They said to him, "Teacher, this woman was caught in the very act of committing adultery. ⁵Now in the law, Moses commanded us to stone such women. So what do you say?" ⁶They said this to test him, so that they could have some charge to bring against him. Jesus bent down and began to write on the ground with his finger. ⁷But when they continued asking him, he straightened up and said to them, "Let the one among you who is without sin be the first to throw a stone at her." ⁸Again he bent down and wrote on the ground. ⁹And in response, they went away one by one, beginning with the elders. So he was left alone with the woman before him. ¹⁰Then Jesus straightened up and said to her, "Woman, where are they? Has no one condemned you?" ¹¹She replied, "No

one, sir." Then Jesus said, "Neither do I condemn you. Go, [and] from now on do not sin
any more."

*After a few moments of quiet reflection on the
passage, consider the following background
information provided in "Setting the Scene."
Continue using the questions in the margins for
personal reflection or for group discussion.*

Setting the Scene

The story of the "Woman Caught in Adultery,"
as this passage is often identified, provides a clear
window into the place of forgiveness in the ministry of Jesus. Adultery was an extraordinarily
serious crime in Jewish law, punishable by death
for the guilty parties. Leviticus 20:10 and Deuteronomy 22:20-26 indicate that the death sen-
tence was applicable to both the man and woman
adulterers, so the Pharisees are not out of line in
questioning whether or not this woman should
be stoned to death. After all, the Torah (the Jewish law revealed in the first five books of Scripture) is not just a series of "do's" and "don'ts"
for the Jewish people; it is the very essence of
their covenantal relationship with God. There is
no such thing as picking and choosing which
parts of the Torah are to be followed.

When the Pharisees ask Jesus, "What do you
say?" about the situation at hand, it is a direct
confrontation as to whether or not Jesus, a Jew,
is faithful to the covenant with God. Will he
follow the sacred law or not? In this situation,
there is no question of determination of guilt.

Have you ever felt trapped in a hostile situation? Does this help you relate to the woman?

After all, this woman was "caught in the very act," and therefore her guilt is indisputable. The real question is how Jesus will respond with regard to her sin. Will Jesus forgive her, or will he stand by the punishment of the law that demands her death?

In legal terms, this is called entrapment. The Pharisees likely have little concern for the life or circumstances of the woman before them. They are focused, as John clearly points out, on bringing her to Jesus "to test him, so that they could have some charge to bring against him."

This is not the only case of the Jewish leaders trying to trap Jesus in order to discredit and eliminate him. For example, the Gospel of Matthew includes a series of such scenes where the Pharisees, Herodians, and Sadducees all conspire to corner Jesus in public scenes of their own making. In Matthew 22:15-17, the Jewish leaders ask about the legality of paying taxes to Caesar; in verses 23-28, they raise a second question about marriage in heaven; and in verses 34-36, the test consists of asking which commandment is considered the greatest. Again, the gospel is clear about the motivation of the religious leaders: they "went off and plotted how they might entrap him in speech" (Matt 22:15).

Scripture scholars largely agree that this passage on the woman caught in adultery was a later addition to John's original gospel, as it is not found in the earliest Greek manuscripts. Although its style and language seem more in keeping with Luke's gospel, theologians believe this early tradition about Jesus was inserted here (and is therefore accepted as canon) because of the context it sets for the subsequent passage of John 8:15-16. In that scene, Jesus confronts the Pharisees and asserts his moral authority: "You judge by appearances, but I do not judge anyone. And even if I should judge, my judgment is valid, because I am not alone, but it is I and the Father who sent me." Jesus' encounter with this adulteress, then, demonstrates the defeat of the Pharisees' moral approach of condemnation, the exposure of their true motivation and duplicity, and the ultimate triumph of Jesus' new law of love and forgiveness.

What are some of the dangers of condemning the behavior of others?

The following information will help you delve more deeply into the story of Jesus forgiving the woman by examining it a few verses at a time.

Understanding the Scene Itself

³**Then the scribes and the Pharisees brought a woman who had been caught in adultery and made her stand in the middle. ⁴They said to him,**

"Teacher, this woman was caught in the very act of committing adultery. ⁵Now in the law, Moses commanded us to stone such women. So what do you say?" ⁶They said this to test him, so that they could have some charge to bring against him.

When the Pharisees reference Mosaic law, the reference is likely either to a passage in Leviticus or Deuteronomy, the two laws that deal directly with adultery, so it serves us well to understand the law at hand. Leviticus states: "If a man commits adultery with his neighbor's wife, both the adulterer and the adulteress shall be put to death" (Lev 20:10). And Deuteronomy distinguishes every possible option:

> If a man is discovered lying with a woman who is married to another, they both shall die, the man who was lying with the woman as well as the woman. . . .
> If there is a young woman, a virgin who is betrothed, and a man comes upon her in the city and lies with her, you shall bring them both out to the gate of the city and there stone them to death. . . . But if it is in the open fields that a man comes upon the betrothed young woman, seizes her and lies with her, only the man who lay with her shall die. You shall do nothing to the young woman, since the young woman is not guilty of a capital offense (Deut 22:22-26).

If the Pharisees have not investigated the reality of the situation, then they themselves are on precarious moral grounds. She may have been, according to the law, seized "in the open fields"

> *Forgiveness is always about relationship and the effects of sin on our relationships.*

and thus "not guilty of a capital offense." On the other hand, if she was "caught in the very act," where is the man? According to the Mosaic law, he is equally guilty.

The markings of sexism, injustice, and bias are evident here, and each of these might be explored in greater depth, but our purpose is to look at this passage through the lens of forgiveness. Forgiveness is always about relationship and the effects of sin on our relationships. So, in this passage, what is the relationship between the woman and the Pharisees? It certainly is not personal. They are using her for their own purposes, manipulating her experiences in order to gain access to a situation that will give them the upper hand over Jesus. They seem to have absolutely no interest in forgiveness whatsoever. Their interest is in sin, and it blinds them. Jesus understands this all too well and refuses to let the Pharisees use this woman—or the law, for that matter—for their own purposes. He sees the woman clearly. And he sees right through the Pharisees.

Have you ever used someone's guilt as an excuse to trap them, not for their own good but for some other reason? How did you become conscious of your motives?

Jesus bent down and began to write on the ground with his finger. 7But when they continued asking him, he straightened up and said to them, "Let the one among you who is without sin be the first to throw a stone at her." 8Again he bent down and wrote on the ground. 9And in response, they went away one by one, beginning with the elders.

How much theological speculation has occurred down the centuries over this last section of verse 6: "Jesus bent down and began to write on the ground with his finger." There's not much to that little verse, but it is filled with intrigue. What is he writing? Who is he writing for? What is the purpose? The earliest interpretations theorize that Jesus was likely just doodling in order to "buy time" and determine how to reply in the situation. A much more compelling theory, however, looks to the Greek word *kategraphen*. This word is not strictly translated "to write" but can be interpreted to mean "to write a record *against* someone or something." An early Armenian

manuscript proposes that Jesus is not doodling in the sand but is writing out plainly, for all to see, the individual sins of all those gathered around.

We cannot know if this is indeed what was happening, but for reflection's sake, let's imagine it was. If we place ourselves in the scene as one of the Pharisees, so convinced of this woman's guilt and the punishment due her, so ready to launch justice as soon as Jesus gets out of the way, so smug in our certainty. . . . If we really sink into that emotional possibility and then let ourselves realize that Jesus is gently but firmly identifying *our own* sinfulness—not in general but in specifics—our response will likely be identical to that of the Pharisees: we too will drop our stones.

"Let the one among you who is without sin be the first to throw a stone." In other words, "Go ahead. Carry out your justice. Enact the law. But only if you are God." In the book of James, we read: "Do not speak evil of one another, brothers. Whoever speaks evil of a brother or judges his brother speaks evil of the law and judges the law. If you judge the law, you are not a doer of the law but a judge. There is one lawgiver and judge who is able to save or to destroy. Who then are you to judge your neighbor?" (James 4:11-12). The law is God's to give and ours to keep. When the Pharisees—or we—begin to use the law as a weapon or a measuring stick or an instrument of power, then God will put us in our proper place.

In Jesus' silent "doodling" response to the situation, every person in that crowd changes course and goes away. In our own prayerful hearing of Jesus' admonition, we are caught up short as we realize that if our own sins were exposed for all to see in vibrant variety, our guilt would be damning. And so, the crowd dissipates. At first, the crowd's vision is focused on the

In your experience, is there a difference between passing judgment on your neighbor and discerning right from wrong? If so, how would you describe this difference?

When personal sinfulness is exposed, even just to yourself, what is your response? Does your embarrassment and humiliation cause you to "go away" from Jesus, or to draw closer in response to his look of forgiveness?

woman; then it seems to turn inward to recognize their own unsuitability to judge her sin. That's an improvement. But surely Jesus would have hoped that in the end they would have turned their sights toward his mercy and opened their eyes to forgiveness. If, in the face of undeniable guilt, our God chooses mercy rather than justice, why would we "go away"?

So he was left alone with the woman before him. [10]Then Jesus straightened up and said to her, "Woman, where are they? Has no one condemned you?" [11]She replied, "No one, sir." Then Jesus said, "Neither do I condemn you. Go, [and] from now on do not sin any more."

How has a growing relationship with Jesus, and an awareness of his love for you, helped to shape your understanding of forgiveness?

When the crowd is completely gone and Jesus and the woman are alone, we see in full clarity how sin and forgiveness operate in the new law of love. Jesus *engages* the woman in conversation. He sees her; he speaks with her. Despite the fact that her sin is egregious; despite the fact that she has not sought forgiveness; despite the fact that she has never professed faith in him as Lord and Savior; despite the fact that he doesn't even know her name—Jesus speaks with her as a woman, as a person. He speaks with her and says quite gently, "I do not condemn you." Forgiveness from Jesus is a result of standing in relationship with him; it is not a result of our worthiness. Jesus forgives this woman without any prelude, prerequisites, or ritual. Jesus *is* forgiveness.

At the same time, Jesus never trivializes or relativizes the primacy of the law. He never says, "Oh, it's ok; don't worry about it," or "Adultery isn't all that bad." He says, "Go on home, and stop it." This is not a condemnation of the woman; this is an exhortation for her fuller and healthier living. Jesus understands and is compassionate toward the weaknesses that lead us into sin, even into terrible sin that destroys family, friends, and full flourishing. Jesus sees sin in all its fullness. He wants to eliminate it from our lives and our living. And he also sees us. *Jesus sees us.*

He reminds us that we are called to something more than what we have become, and he reminds us that in essence our identity is wrapped up in belonging to him. When we can remember this, we are more likely to "live in a manner worthy of the call [we] have received," as Paul would say (Eph 4:1).

Receiving forgiveness from Christ will change our lives. I imagine it changed the life of this "adulterous woman." Relationship with Jesus will help us recognize and admit to our own sinfulness and know that we must make a choice. Remember the reference the Pharisees made to the demands of the Jewish law in the Torah? Jesus seems to beat them at their own game by

What factors make it difficult to accept forgiveness? And what factors make it difficult to offer?

living out a subsequent passage from Deuter-onomy: "I call heaven and earth today to witness against you: I have set before you life and death, the blessing and the curse. Choose life, then, that you and your descendants may live, by loving the LORD, your God, obeying his voice, and hold-ing fast to him" (Deut 30:19-20).

Our choice for life comes from relationship with Jesus—because of who *he* is and not because of what *we've* done. Forgiveness, not condemna-tion, is what he offers us. Will we receive it?

Praying the Word / Sacred Reading

- *Spend a few moments recalling a past sin that caused you to fear God's condemna-tion.*
- *Read the exchange between Jesus and the adulterous woman three times through, and then replace the word "woman" with your own name as you read it one final time.*
- *Consider either taking your personal ex-perience to the sacrament of reconciliation or journaling about the experience of Jesus' forgiveness.*

Living the Word

Identify a person in your workplace or family who has hurt you in a way that makes it easy to judge him or her. In the next week or so, deliberately put yourself in that person's path to engage him or her in a conversation, even if it is a casual one. Ask Jesus to give you his eyes to see the person, and focus on looking him or her directly in the eye when you speak. When the conversation is finished, ask Jesus to help you see the person as he does and to help you forgive him or her.

Sharing in the Mission of Jesus

Ask God's direction and understanding as you prayerfully read a portion of John 21, the post-resurrection encounter between Peter and Jesus.

John 21:14-19

¹⁴This was now the third time Jesus was revealed to his disciples after being raised from the dead.

¹⁵When they had finished breakfast, Jesus said to Simon Peter, "Simon, son of John, do you love me more than these?" He said to him, "Yes, Lord, you know that I love you." He said to him, "Feed my lambs." ¹⁶He then said to him a second time, "Simon, son of John, do you love me?" He said to him, "Yes, Lord, you know that I love you." He said to him, "Tend my sheep." ¹⁷He said to him the third time, "Simon, son of John, do you love me?" Peter was distressed that he had said to him a third time, "Do you love me?" and he said to him, "Lord, you know everything; you know that I love you." [Jesus] said to him, "Feed my sheep. ¹⁸Amen, amen, I say to

you, when you were younger, you used to dress yourself and go where you wanted; but when you grow old, you will stretch out your hands, and someone else will dress you and lead you where you do not want to go." ¹⁹He said this signifying by what kind of death he would glorify God. And when he had said this, he said to him, "Follow me."

> *The information provided in "Setting the Scene" will situate the passage within the larger message of John's final chapters.*

Setting the Scene

This passage comes from the very last chapter of John's gospel. It is a story of the apostles interacting and continuing to learn from the risen Jesus about what it means to be a resurrection people. Sometimes those post-resurrection lessons for the disciples lightened the heart and filled the spirit. What relief to hear "Peace be with you" in Luke's account (Luke 24:36). And what hope is born from the assurance ". . . behold, I am with you always" in Matthew's account (Matt 28:20). But sometimes what the apostles learned is difficult, as in John 21, and those lessons reach into our own discipleship even today. These lessons are a personal challenge, costing us something.

The risen Christ still bears the wounds of the crucifixion, and the hands that reach out to bless the disciples are nail-scarred. The resurrected Jesus reveals a God who forgives. And the resurrected Jesus also shows us what it means to forgive as a

How do you picture Jesus in his appearances to the disciples after his resurrection?

human being. Indeed, Jesus shows us that to be fully human, to be his followers, we must forgive.

The last two chapters of John's gospel are filled with stories of Jesus' resurrection appearances—to Mary Magdalene, to the disciples in the Upper Room, to Thomas, and to Peter and friends as they are out fishing (unsuccessfully) one morning. The conversation between Peter and Jesus considered here immediately follows Jesus' appearance on the beach when he instructs the men to throw the nets off the other side of the boat in order to make a catch. When they do so and come up with more fish than they can manage, Peter immediately recognizes this stranger on the beach to be Jesus, and they return to the shore where they find that Jesus has prepared breakfast for them. This gospel passage then picks up with the conversation in which Jesus engages Peter about love and lambs. At first glance, it may not seem that this exchange has much connection

with the virtue of forgiveness, but Jesus' thrice-repeated question to Peter, "Do you love me?" can be heard as a loving echo and forgiving balm to Peter's thrice-repeated denial of "I tell you I do not know the man" in Jerusalem on the night before the crucifixion (see John 18:15-27).

Peter's "mess-ups" are some of the more obvious, consistent, and personal in the gospels. After having the faith to get out of a boat and walk on water toward Jesus, Peter hesitates and starts to sink, evoking from Jesus the response, "O you of little faith, why did you doubt?" (Matt 14:31). When Peter tries to defend Jesus in the Garden of Gethsemane and lashes out with a sword, striking the high priest's slave, Jesus rebukes him, "Put your sword into its scabbard. Shall I not drink the cup that the Father gave me?" (John 18:11). And perhaps worst of all was when Jesus characterized Peter as being in league with the Evil One by saying, "Get behind me, Satan! You are an obstacle to me. You are thinking not as God does, but as human beings do" (Matt 16:23). Of course, each of these incidents had a context that might be understandable, but the fact of the matter is that Peter wasn't the perfect follower. His words, his thoughts, and his actions at least occasionally required Jesus' (and I daresay the other apostles') forgiveness.

Considering how the gospels portray Peter, what is your impression of him? Would you choose him as a friend?

When Jesus forgives Peter, it comes at a personal cost to Peter. "Do you realize what I have done for you? . . . I have given you a model to follow, so that as I have done for you, you should also do" (John 13:12, 15). Forgiveness is a gift, freely given, but it is given to us that we might learn how to turn around and give it to others. "Without cost you have received; without cost you are to give" (Matt 10:8). And how often must we do this? We know the answer: "Not seven times but seventy-seven times" (Matt 18:22). In other words: don't keep count. Just keep forgiving. This is what it means to respond with our life to Jesus' invitation: "Follow me."

When has a personal experience of being forgiven helped you to be more forgiving to someone else?

John 21:14-19 will be examined a few verses at a time to allow for deeper understanding. The questions will continue to guide your reflection or discussion.

Understanding the Scene Itself

¹⁴**This was now the third time Jesus was revealed to his disciples after being raised from the dead. ¹⁵When they had finished breakfast, Jesus said to Simon Peter, "Simon, son of John, do you love me more than these?" He said to him, "Yes, Lord, you know that I love you." He said to him, "Feed my lambs."**

Scripture scholars believe that chapter 21 of John's gospel was added after the original gospel was completed, written by the Johannine community as their confirmation of the historicity of the resurrection. The details would therefore be quite purposeful, asserting something vital to the understanding of what it meant for early Christians to follow the Way of Jesus.

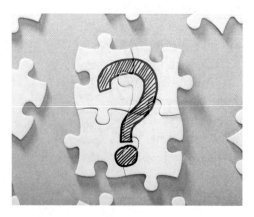

The question posed by Jesus to Peter, "Do you love me more than these?" is ambiguous in its object. What or who are "these"? Did Jesus mean, "Do you love me more than these things (i.e., your livelihood, your friends, your comfort)?" Or did he mean,

"Do you love me more than these other disciples love me?" Or did he mean, "Do you love me more than you love these others?" It is unclear from the text, and therefore the reader is left to ponder for herself or himself. Regardless, the question is a personal one.

Prior to this episode, the last direct personal interaction recorded between Jesus and Peter was in the Garden of Gethsemane (see John 18) when Peter cut off the ear of the high priest's slave in protest against Jesus' arrest. After that, Peter followed at a distance to the courtyard of the high priest where Jesus was being questioned, and it was in that courtyard that he denied even knowing Jesus. At the sound of the cock's crow, Jesus' prediction of Peter's threefold denial was affirmed, and Peter disappears from the gospel until the morning of the resurrection.

So when the resurrected Jesus asks, "Simon, son of John, do you love me more than . . . ?" we must understand that this is the first one-on-one conversation recorded between Peter and Jesus after the courtyard denial. Jesus doesn't ask, "Simon, son of John, why did you do that?" or say, "Chosen Apostle Simon, you blew it," or even, "I forgive you, Simon." Rather, he puts the onus on Peter and makes himself vulnerable to Peter's response—*again*. Jesus' question is, "Do *you* love *me*?" not "Can *I* keep loving *you*?" Forgiveness for Peter's denial is implicit in the mere question posed by Jesus—a question that doesn't simply ask, "Do you love me?" but "Do you love me more than . . ." This is Peter's opportunity to make an honest and direct self-assessment and

Have you previously considered the many ways of understanding what Jesus meant when he asked Peter to compare his love to "these"? What new insights have you gained?

How is the selflessness of Jesus expressed in the way Jesus opens his conversation with Peter? What role does selflessness play in forgiveness?

decision about his discipleship. This is no longer the inviting Jesus who calls him away from his fishing profession or his anticipated future. This is a resurrected Jesus who calls him into a deeper relationship with himself—one that has weathered the storm of violence, fear, and betrayal; one that requires a renewal.

Peter's response? "Yes, Lord, you know that I love you." Peter, for all his flaws and foibles, knows who Jesus is. And he admits who he himself is as well. Maybe Peter's response could be characterized like this: "Yes, Lord. You know me, and you have always known what I'm capable of. Of course you know what's in my heart right now, after everything. And you love me in spite of myself. You know how much I love you. And you know how much I need you." Jesus responds not with an acceptance of Peter's apology or an admonition to him to repent, but with a commission: "Feed my lambs." Peter—fumbling, frail Peter—is commissioned, by him who

When has an act of forgiveness in your life (given or received) led to a new sense of purpose?

overcame sin and death, to be the successor of the Good Shepherd himself.

¹⁶He then said to him a second time, "Simon, son of John, do you love me?" He said to him, "Yes, Lord, you know that I love you." He said to him, "Tend my sheep."

The question comes a second time. What are we to make of this, a question that Jesus repeats but this time without the scale of comparison? The second question isn't about whether Peter's love is "more than these," but rather is a basic question that seeks a profession of love, a confirmation. How often we require this second assurance. In our own lives, we likely profess our love for Jesus in moments of deep prayer, sincerely offering our gratitude and commitment to him. "I love you, and I am forever grateful for your love for me." Our hearts can utter this prayer in moments of peacefulness, in moments of joy, even in moments of heartache or despair. The prayer is surely sincere and full and ready to listen. A good question to ask, however, is whether or not it's routine.

When Jesus asks Peter a second time, "Do you love me?" we may be caught off guard. Did he not hear Peter's answer? Did he not hear *our* answer? "Yes, Lord, you know that I love you," we say with a bit of confusion, a smidge of worry, and a readiness to prove our love. "Yes, Lord, I love you." This second response is not routine; it has been made, in its repetition, deliberate, and in that deliberateness it feels a bit

> What would be your response to someone who asked you a second time, "Do you love me?" after you had affirmed your love in the first place?

weightier. "I do love you, Lord. I love who you are, and I love our relationship. I am here." What is Jesus' response to that more thoughtful, more purposeful affirmation of love—both Peter's and our own? A confirmation of what the task is before us: "Tend my sheep." Go. Look after those entrusted to you. Don't assume that your love for me stays in the church. It must go forth in service and in seeking out the lost. Go.

¹⁷**He said to him the third time, "Simon, son of John, do you love me?" Peter was distressed that he had said to him a third time, "Do you love me?" and he said to him, "Lord, you know everything; you know that I love you." [Jesus] said to him, "Feed my sheep. ¹⁸Amen, amen, I say to you, when you were younger, you used to dress yourself and go where you wanted; but when you grow old, you will stretch out your hands, and someone else will dress you and lead you where you do not want to go." ¹⁹He said this signifying by what kind of death he would glorify God. And when he had said this, he said to him, "Follow me."**

A third time? What is happening here? Let's take a moment to study the actual text of this passage, because the words Jesus uses in posing these questions to Peter are purposeful. In Greek, there are multiple words that are translated into the English word "love." *Agape* is unconditional, self-sacrificial love, whereas *philia* is affectionate, friendship love. In this conversation, the first time Jesus asks Peter the question, he says,

"Simon, son of John, do you *'agape'* me?" Peter replies, "Yes, Lord, you know that I *'philia'* you." That seems like kind of a weak answer to Jesus' question!

In using the word *agape*, Jesus is asking Peter if he loves him enough to suffer, to give without counting the cost, to love unconditionally. Peter's response seems to be, "Well, I love you enough to be your really good friend." So Jesus asks a second time: "Simon, son of John, do you *'agape'* me?" And Peter replies again: "Yes, Lord, you know that I *'philia'* you." Consider what this would feel like in a conversation you might have with a friend—or spouse. Question: "Do you love me enough to give up some of your own self-interest, my beloved?" Answer: "I have great affection for you, my friend." Where might that relationship go from there?

What is difficult about "upping" our love for Jesus from friendship to self-sacrificial love?

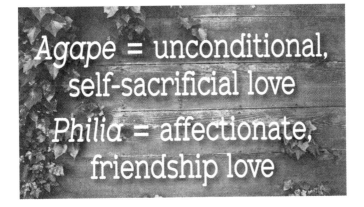

Agape = unconditional, self-sacrificial love
Philia = affectionate, friendship love

In the third posing of the question, Jesus changes the word he uses. The third time, Jesus says, "Simon, Son of John, do you *'philia'* me?" and Peter becomes upset, answering that Jesus certainly knows that he has *philia* for him! Peter cannot bring himself to commit to *agape* in this exchange. Even with Jesus' forgiveness of his denial, even with Jesus' commission to take on the ministry of shepherd, Peter cannot profess *agape* love, and he becomes distressed at Jesus' question even when Jesus "lowers the bar" and refers to *philia* love.

What situation are you aware of that is inviting you to imitate Jesus and meet another person where they are rather than where you wish them to be? What will you do to create such an opportunity?

The tender forgiveness of the resurrected Jesus at this point in the exchange is exquisite. Jesus does not rebuke Peter for his "lesser" *philia* love. Instead he meets him where he is and asks him to make a full-throated commitment to *philia*. And when Peter assents, Jesus gives Peter a very gentle explanation of what following the cruci-fied and risen Christ will entail. Love for him—even simple friendship with him—will require sacrifice. Peter's *philia* will become *agape*. In-deed, when we commit to a relationship with Jesus, we will find ourselves in situations and circumstances that we might not have chosen for ourselves. Our faith will cost us something; this is the price of true love.

Jesus doesn't end this extended give-and-take conversation with a question; he ends it with a command. Jesus says, not just to Peter but to you and to me: "Follow me."

Praying the Word / Sacred Reading

Take a quiet moment in a place where you will not be interrupted for at least ten minutes. Settle into the quiet, and then hear Jesus ask you the question, "Do you love me?"

Before you answer, just absorb the question. Hear him repeat, "Do you love me?" Imagine his eyes looking at you as he speaks to you. Imagine his facial expression. Try to hear the tone of his voice. Then, without using too many words, answer Jesus with the response of your heart.

Continue to imagine his eyes and his facial expression as you answer. As you end your period of prayer, hear him say gently, quietly, "Follow me."

Living the Word

Choose someone in your everyday life who you feel needs to be reminded of his or her "lovableness." Write the person a note or engage in a purposeful conversation, sharing your thoughts about what makes that person special. If he or she has a hard time receiving your words, try a second time without laughing it off. Make your comments specific, genuine, and tender.